Pr

Seeking God, in a world darkened by sin, is a struggle. Seeking Christ, the chief cornerstone, amidst the countless stones of life is a great challenge. These Bible studies have allowed this search for truth to be that much easier, and have been a guiding light to professionals like myself working within the downtown Calgary area. The application of biblical truth to everyday workday situations has provided support, encouragement, and proof that God is truly present with us while we partake in our work and in our everyday tasks. These Bible studies have led to the development of strong friendships amongst the participants, and lifelong friends in Christ.

I would highly recommend these studies to the individual who desires to take their relationship with God to the next level, and integrate the Lord of Heaven and Earth into a new area of their life.

Caleb
Financial Advisor

These Bible studies have helped me grow spiritually and have been a great tool to help facilitate discussion at our small group. They relate well to everyday life and are applicable for any Christian or individual who wants to learn more about the Christian faith.

Andrew
Finance

MARKETPLACE **BIBLE STUDIES** *2*

Gifted TO DO
OUR WORK

JAMES **BRUYN**

GIFTED TO DO OUR WORK
Copyright © 2015 by James Bruyn
Photos copyright Susan Bruyn

ISBN: 978-1-4866-0974-1   Printed in Canada

Word Alive Press
131 Cordite Road, Winnipeg, MB R3W 1S1
www.wordalivepress.ca

MIX
Paper from
responsible sources
FSC® C016245

WORD ALIVE
— P R E S S —

FSC
www.fsc.org

Library and Archives Canada Cataloguing in Publication

Bruyn, James, 1964-, author
      Gifted to do our work : marketplace Bible studies. Book 2 / James Bruyn.

Issued in print and electronic formats.
ISBN 978-1-4866-0974-1 (paperback).--ISBN 978-1-4866-0975-8 (pdf).--
ISBN 978-1-4866-0976-5 (html).--ISBN 978-1-4866-0977-2 (epub)

      1. Work--Religious aspects--Christianity. 2. Work--Biblical teaching.
3. Vocation--Christianity. I. Title.

BT738.5.B782 2015   248.8'8   C2015-904202-X
                                                                C2015-904203-8

Acknowledgements

God used the Scriptures in these studies to sustain me, to strengthen me, and to give me the courage to stand firm in my faith. It is my privilege to share with you what God has been teaching me through many years of life experiences in the workplace.

I would like to thank my wonderful wife Susan and three children who have constantly encouraged me and faithfully supported me.

Twenty-five years ago, Rich, when you set me on this path, neither of us knew what God was preparing me for. Thank you for your advice.

For Mark, Doug, Rainer, and Matt, thank you for believing in me, and encouraging me and holding me up in prayer.

For Roanna, Nathan, and Andrew, thank you for allowing me to journey with you as you launched your Bible study at your workplace. It has been exciting to watch what God has been doing at your workplace.

TABLE OF CONTENTS

Introduction   ix

How to Use These Studies   xi

1. Gifted to Do Our Work   1
   How do we faithfully use the gifts God has given us at work?

2. Hearing God's Voice in the Workplace   9
   *How do we discern what God is saying to us in our
   work situations?*

3. Working Wholeheartedly...for God   15
   *What does it mean that we are doing the will of God
   when we're doing our jobs?*

4. Working with Integrity   21
   *What are the risks and benefits of being identified as
   Christian at work?*

5. Standing Firm in Our Faith   27
   What cost are we willing to pay to stand firm in our faith?

6. Preparing for the Future   35
   What could we do to prepare for tomorrow?

7. Trusting in God   41
   *When our circumstances change at work, can we trust
   in God?*

8. Self-Reliance   47
   Who are you trusting to see you through?

For Further Reflection   55

For Further Study   59

About the Author   61

Introduction

How has God prepared us for our work?

We work in environments where trusting in God and acknowledging that God has gifted us to do our work seems irrelevant. Sometimes it feels like the cost of working with integrity, and standing firm in our faith, is too high a price to pay.

God has blessed you with the skills and abilities so that you can make a unique contribution to this world, and God's kingdom, through your work. You can trust God in every situation you find yourself at work. He will provide you with the strength and the courage to honor him in everything that you do at work. Monday Mornings are glorious opportunities for you to see God at work in your workplace and wherever you go.

This is the second in a series of Bible studies designed to provide an opportunity for you to carve time out of your schedule and gather with others to read the Bible together and discuss what it means to integrate your faith into your daily work lives. Embark on this journey of discovery in your own devotions, or share this journey with a friend or mentor, or with a group of co-workers or your small group.

As you go through these studies, affirm one another for the precious talents, gifts, wisdom, knowledge, and understanding God has given you. May you hear God speak to you through his word. Remind each other that when we do our work, we're serving the Lord. May nobody be able to find fault in how you do your job or your attitude towards your work. May God's name be glorified on earth and in heaven.

How to Use These Studies

If you're leading a small group using these studies, feel free to adapt them to the unique style of leading and communicating that God has blessed you with. As you introduce a study, share your own story about the topic. Your story will help your small group relate to the topic, and help foster a safe place where your group members can share their joys and struggles in the workplace.

The people in your small group will get the most value out of these studies if each is given a chance to share their thoughts on every question. One effective way to use these studies is as follows:

1. The group members introduce themselves and answer the ice breaker question included with each study.

2. The leader shares his or her own introduction to the topic.

3. One or more people read aloud the Scripture for the study. You may find it helpful to have the Scripture read aloud twice.

4. Split the group into smaller groups of three or four. This allows everybody to respond to each of the questions.

5. About ten minutes before the end of the study, invite everybody to come together and share something they learned.

6. Ask for prayer requests, and take a few minutes to pray.

Feel free to use your own ice breaker questions. If the people in your group have already begun to build relationships, you could skip over the ice breaker altogether. If you wish, you can incorporate the ice breaker question as the first question in the study. People like to give fairly lengthy stories to the ice breaker questions, so as your group grows be careful that you don't end up spending too much time on the ice breaker question.

Each study includes an application in the Applying God's Truth section. Encourage people to find a partner in the group or outside the group to share how the application is working out in their life.

You may find it helpful to share the leadership of these studies with two or three co-workers or friends. Then when you have another commitment during the Bible study time, your co-worker can lead the study in your place. In addition, try and find someone in your group who God has blessed with the gift of a gatherer or organizer who can send out weekly email invites, book the room, and look after the logistics.

Chapter 1

Gifted to Do Our Work

How Do We Faithfully Use the Gifts God Has Given Us at Work?

Whatever you do, whether in word or deed, do it all in the name of the Lord Jesus, giving thanks to God the Father through him.
—Colossians 3:17

> *Ice Breaker:*
> What was the best job you've ever had, and why?

IN THE OLD TESTAMENT, GOD GIVES US GLIMPSES INTO THE LIVES of men and women who were filled with the Spirit of God. We meet mighty leaders like Moses, Joseph, and Gideon. We also meet talented tradesmen and women who sewed the garments for the priests, who built the tabernacle, who farmed, raised cattle, herded sheep and did countless other jobs.

Each of them was chosen by God for a specific task. Even before they were born, God had planned for each of these men to be born with their unique personality, learning styles, and interests. God filled each of them with the Spirit of God and with wisdom, understanding, and knowledge to lead, to design, to build, and to serve at that particular time.

This same God has blessed you and me with understanding to solve the inevitable problems that arise in our jobs. He's blessed us with the knowledge to do what is necessary to fulfill the requirements of our jobs, and he's blessed us with the wisdom to learn the skills and teach others the skills to do our jobs with excellence.

Each of our abilities is a precious gift God uniquely chose to bestow upon us for God's honor and glory.

EXODUS 35:30–35 (SEE ALSO EXODUS 31:1–11)

Then Moses said to the Israelites, "See, the Lord has chosen Bezalel son of Uri, the son of Hur, of the tribe of Judah, and he has filled him with the Spirit of God, with wisdom, with understanding, with knowledge and with all kinds of skills—to make artistic designs for work in gold, silver and bronze, to cut and set stones, to work in wood and to engage in all kinds of artistic crafts. And he has given both him and Oholiab son of Ahisamak, of the tribe of Dan, the ability to teach others. He has filled them with skill to do all kinds of work as engravers, designers, embroiderers in blue, purple and scarlet yarn and fine linen, and weavers—all of them skilled workers and designers.

MATTHEW 25:21

Well done, good and faithful servant! You have been faithful with a few things; I will put you in charge of many things. Come and share your master's happiness!

JAMES 1:5–6

If any of you lacks wisdom, you should ask God, who gives generously to all without finding fault, and it will be given to you. But when you ask, you must believe and not doubt, because the one who doubts is like a wave of the sea, blown and tossed by the wind.

JAMES 3:17

But the wisdom that comes from heaven is first of all pure; then peace–loving, considerate, submissive, full of mercy and good fruit, impartial and sincere.

JAMES 3:13–16

But if you harbor bitter envy and selfish ambition in your hearts, do not boast about it or deny the truth. Such "wisdom" does not come down from heaven but is earthly, unspiritual, demonic. For where you have envy and selfish ambition, there you find disorder and every evil practice.

STUDY QUESTIONS

1. Thinking of ways that don't include explicitly or verbally acknowledging God, how would your co-workers recognize the Spirit of God in you:

   a) When you're doing work you enjoy?

   b) When you're doing work you don't enjoy, or weren't trained for?

2. What does it mean to you to know that God has filled you with the wisdom, understanding, and knowledge to do your work? What difference does that make in the way you approach your job?

3. We see the work of our co-workers and others, and their work is good and appears blessed by God, and it benefits other people. How do we explain this?

4. How do you make sure that you're faithfully using God's gifts of wisdom, knowledge, and understanding in your job (both during the tasks you enjoy and those you don't)?

5. For those of you who are feeling like round pegs in square holes, how do you find ways to faithfully use the skills, wisdom, knowledge, and understanding God has given you while you prepare for the future round hole that God has planned for you?

6. Share a story of how God has provided wisdom to you in the past. How could God provide wisdom to you in your current circumstances?

7. Share an example of somebody who communicates their wisdom in a manner you like, and an example of somebody who communicates their wisdom in an offensive manner.

8. How can you share your wisdom with others in a way that is peace-loving, considerate, submissive, full of mercy and good fruit, impartial and sincere?

9. Why would you or have you given up on envy and self-ish ambition to show godly wisdom? Has there been

a time when demonstrating godly wisdom hasn't resulted in financial reward or increased status at work? Why is it worthwhile to show godly wisdom at work?

SUMMARY

COLOSSIANS 3:17

And whatever you do, whether in word or deed, do it all in the name of the Lord Jesus, giving thanks to God the Father through him.

God delights over you as each facet of your life so wonderfully reflects His glory. God rejoices over you! He sees his love sparkling as you use your spiritual gifts. He sees his love sparkling as you use the talents and skills he gave you.

Each of our abilities and talents and spiritual gifts is a precious gift God uniquely chose to bestow upon us. Our abilities and talents are not something to be despised or abused. They are not meant to be minimized in comparison to our Spiritual gifts.

Be the best you that you can be today! That is how God has gifted you, how God has created you, and who God has called you to be.

APPLYING GOD'S TRUTHS

What's one challenge, problem, or issue at work that you don't know how to solve right now? Ask God for wisdom to solve this problem.

What is one thing at work that you find boring and uninteresting? Thank God for giving you the wisdom, understanding, and knowledge to do this task with excellence.

PRAYER

Father, thank you for the unique personalities, learning styles, and interests that you have blessed each one of us with. Thank you for the wisdom, understanding, and knowledge that you have blessed us with so that we can do our jobs with excellence. Help us to do our work in such a way that your name is glorified.

Help us, Lord, to do our work in a way that allows our co-workers to recognize your Spirit in us. Help us to be faithful to you in everything we do at work. Forgive us for the times we have been jealous of our co-workers. Help us to encourage our co-workers to use the skills and gifts that you have blessed them with. Amen.

Chapter 2

Hearing God's Voice in the Workplace

HOW DO WE DISCERN WHAT GOD IS SAYING TO US IN OUR WORK SITUATIONS?

My sheep listen to my voice; I know them, and they follow me.
I give them eternal life, and they shall never perish;
no one will snatch them out of my hand.
—John 10:27-28

Ice Breaker:
What was your very first job? What's one thing
you remember or learned from that job?

THERE ARE A MYRIAD OF VOICES AND CONVERSATIONS HAPPENING in the workplace. In the midst of all these voices, how do we discern what God is saying to us?

There's so much going on in our lives that it's easy to be distracted from hearing God's voice. We easily get wrapped up in the enjoyment of a task or the success of completing a large project or winning a major deal; or we get caught up in the everyday routine of life; or we feel unappreciated, manipulated, and used. At other times we totally mess up. As we focus on all that's going on around us, God's voice seems to become harder and harder to hear. How do we hear what God is saying to us in the middle of everything that's going on?

JOHN 10:1–5, 27–29

[Jesus said, "I tell you the truth,] anyone who does not enter the sheep pen by the gate, but climbs in by some other way, is a thief and a robber. The one who enters by the gate is the shepherd of the sheep. The gatekeeper opens the gate for him, and the sheep listen to his voice. He calls his own sheep by name and leads them out. When he has brought out all his own, he goes on ahead of them, and his sheep follow him because they

know his voice. But they will never follow a stranger; in fact, they will run away from him because they do not recognize a stranger's voice."

My sheep listen to my voice; I know them, and they follow me. I give them eternal life, and they shall never perish; no one will snatch them out of my hand. My Father, who has given them to me, is greater than all; no one can snatch them out of my Father's hand.

STUDY QUESTIONS

1. What does God's voice communicate? Try to give specific examples.

2. How do you know when you are or aren't listening to God's voice?

3. When you hear God's voice, what do you hear and understand and obey (or ignore, or disobey)? Why? What does it mean to you to obey God?

4. What does it mean to you that Jesus knows your name?

5. When Jesus the good shepherd goes before us and calls us to follow him, we don't know where he will lead us. What *do* we know that gives us the confidence to follow him?

6. How can God speak to us? Can God speak through the people we work with, and our circumstances at

work? When people correct you, or when people praise you for what you do, is God speaking through them? Share an example of how God has spoken to you through other people at work.

7. Many things in life distract us from hearing God's voice and following God. What are some things at work that distract you from hearing God's voice, or drown out God's voice?

8. We regularly hear things at work about people, or change in the organization, and we have no clue what the impact will be on us. We tend in these situations to be afraid of the unknown, and often we sit around for hours discussing and dissecting the change, speculating about what's next. In the middle of these changes, announcements of change, or rumors of pending change, what is God's voice saying to us (or is God speaking at all)?

SUMMARY

PSALM 119:64–73 (NLT)

O Lord, your unfailing love fills the earth; teach me your decrees. You have done many good things for me, Lord, just as you promised. I believe in your commands; now teach me good judgment and knowledge. I used to wander off until you disciplined me; but now I closely follow your word. You are good and do only good; teach me your decrees. Arrogant people smear me with lies, but in truth I obey your commandments with all my heart. Their hearts are dull and stupid, but I delight in your instructions. My suffering was good for me, for it taught me to pay attention to your decrees. Your instructions are more valuable to me than millions in gold and silver. You made me; you created me. Now give me the sense to follow your commands.

APPLYING GOD'S TRUTH

As you hear and experience things at work this week, listen to hear what God is saying to you through the Bible, your co-workers, and work experiences. Make a list of what you have heard and share it with a friend.

PRAYER

Thank you, Father, for your gift of eternal life, and that we are safe in the nail-scarred hands of your son Jesus. In the middle of all the change that is happening at work, we rejoice that you are unchanging.

Father, in the midst of all the noise around us, help us to hear your voice. Keep us from being deceived and led astray by other voices that call out to us. Forgive us for the times when we have not listened to your voice or have been distracted.

Lord, you have done so many good things for us, and your unfailing love fills the earth. Teach us your decrees. We need your wisdom so that we can do our work with excellence. We need your wisdom so that we can discern truth from error. Now grant us the common sense to follow your commands at work and at home and wherever we are. Amen.

Chapter 3

Working Wholeheartedly... for God

WHAT DOES IT MEAN THAT WE ARE DOING THE WILL OF GOD WHEN WE'RE DOING OUR JOBS?

Whatever you do, work at it with all your heart, as working for the Lord, not for human masters
—Colossians 3:23

Ice Breaker:
Who was your favorite manager? Why?

SO MUCH WORK TO DO, TOO LITTLE TIME TO DO IT. AN IMPORTANT deadline is looming and the little clock at the bottom right corner of the screen says you're going to be late to get your child to hockey. Another day, and in another job your work is finished by noon, and you hang around bored watching the clock slowly change until you can sneak out just a little early.

Your manager comes down the hallway, and in front of all your friends announces what a great job you did, and that she's giving you a big bonus. All your friends gather round and cheer for you. Another day, and in another job, you wrap up your presentation to your manager in a meeting you found out about five minutes before it started. Your manager tears a strip off of you for being ill-prepared, and threatens to fire you.

Another day, and in another job, you're constantly looking over your shoulder afraid that your micro-manager boss is not going to approve of the way you're dealing with customers, and you wonder why you're even bothering to do this job.

We find ourselves in great work situations and in horrible work situations, and in everything in between. In each of these situations, Paul tells us in Ephesians 6:6 to *"do* [our] *work as slaves of Christ, doing the will of God from* [our] *heart."* What does it mean that our jobs are where we serve the Lord, and not just a means of paying the bills? What does it mean that we are doing the will of God when we're working, and not just putting in time until we get to heaven?

EPHESIANS 6:5-9

Slaves, obey your earthly masters with respect and fear, and with sincerity of heart, just as you would obey Christ. Obey them not only to win their favor when their eye is on you, but as slaves of Christ, doing the will of God from your heart. Serve wholeheartedly, as if you were serving the Lord, not people, because you know that the Lord will reward each one for whatever good they do, whether they are slave or free.
And masters, treat your slaves in the same way. Do not threaten them, since you know that he who is both their Master and yours is in heaven, and there is no favoritism with him.

STUDY QUESTIONS

1. In some jobs, we work for managers who are supportive, pleasant, and easy to work with. At other times, we work for managers who make our lives difficult. Share an example of how you've obeyed difficult or pleasant managers with respect and fear and with sincerity of heart just as you would obey Christ.

2. Share some examples of when you find it hard to obey your manager.

3. When you talk with people about "knowing the will of God" for your life or "doing the will of God," what topics do you discuss? For example, maybe you've discussed who God wants you to marry, or where God wants you to live. How do the topics you've discussed compare to the phrase "doing the will of God" from this passage?

4. When you're at work, how do you reflect that you are doing the will of God from your heart? (Think about your attitude, how you use your time, the quality of your work, and how you respond to your manager.)

5. When is it hard to do your job in a way that shows you are doing the will of God from your heart?

6. There are times when our managers don't recognize our contribution to the organization, or they give us roles that don't utilize the gifts and abilities God has blessed us with. There are days when we have spare time on our hands, and other days when we have too much to do. Our employers can have policies that are annoying or inconvenient.

    What difference does it make in the way you approach your work, and your attitude in these situations, knowing that you're serving the Lord and not just working for a living or serving your manager or your company?

7. Paul says, *"Masters, treat your slaves in the same way."* How do you think Paul meant for you to treat the people who work for you or with you?

SUMMARY

God places a choice before each one of us: we can choose to do our work as if we are slaves of Christ serving the Lord, or we can choose to do our work to make money for ourselves, or to please others. When we choose to do our work as service unto God, we will find true satisfaction and contentment.

Doing our work as service unto God does not mean we will always enjoy what we're doing. It doesn't mean we will always be treated with respect or kindness. However, when we do our work as service unto God, we know that our ultimate reward comes from God.

APPLYING GOD'S TRUTHS

What do you need as a physical reminder to help you remember that you're doing your work as service unto God?

PRAYER

Father, working with other people is hard sometimes. Some days our work is enjoyable, and some days it is challenging. Help us to keep our eyes fixed on you, the source of our faith and the one who brings our faith to maturity.

Lord, we look forward to the day when we will be with you in Heaven, and these light and momentary troubles will have passed away and we will have achieved an eternal glory that outweighs them all. Amen.

Chapter 4
Working with Integrity

WHAT ARE THE RISKS AND BENEFITS OF BEING IDENTIFIED AS CHRISTIAN AT WORK?

He has shown you, O man, what is good.
And what does the Lord require of you?
To act justly and to love mercy and to
walk humbly with your God.
—Micah 6:8

Ice Breaker:
When you were a child, how did you try to get
out of doing what your parents asked?

WHAT IS OUR REPUTATION AT WORK? WHAT DO OTHER PEOPLE SAY about us? What, if anything, distinguishes those of us who are Christians? Do we live as children of God only when we're doing church activities, or are we also children of God at work?

Daniel distinguished himself while working in a role that enhanced and progressed the kingdom of Babylon. The Babylonians did not acknowledge or comply with the values and sovereignty of the Kingdom of God, or give assent to Daniel's faith or worldview. Daniel was far away from his family and the temple. Yet the other leaders of Babylon could not find anything to accuse Daniel of. Can the same be said about us at our jobs?

DANIEL 6:1–5

It pleased Darius to appoint 120 satraps to rule throughout the kingdom, with three administrators over them, one of whom was Daniel. The satraps were made accountable to them so that the king might not suffer loss. Now Daniel so distinguished himself among the administrators and the satraps by his exceptional qualities that the king planned to set him over the whole kingdom. At this, the administrators and the satraps tried to find grounds for charges against Daniel in his conduct of government affairs, but they were unable to do so. They could find no corruption in him, because he was trustworthy and neither corrupt nor negligent. Finally these men said, "We will never find any basis for charges against this man Daniel unless it has something to do with the law of his God."

ISAIAH 50:10–11

Who among you fears the Lord and obeys the word of his servant? Let the one who walks in the dark, who has no light, trust in the name of the Lord and rely on their God. But now, all you who light fires and provide yourselves with flaming torches, go, walk in the light of your fires and of the torches you have set ablaze. This is what you shall receive from my hand: You will lie down in torment.

STUDY QUESTIONS

1. What is Daniel's reputation according to this passage? What's your reputation at work?

2. Working for a government that did not acknowledge or comply with the values of the Kingdom of God, or give assent to his faith or worldview, why might Daniel have chosen to work with integrity? What reasons might Daniel have had to be untrustworthy, corrupt, or negligent? Why would Daniel have chosen not to work this way?

3. How would you characterize Daniel's relationship with God? How might Daniel's relationship with God have impacted his behavior? How could you cultivate that kind of relationship?

4. What about you? What is your reputation in your job? Why have you chosen to live and work the way you do?

5. What issues, or pressures, or kinds of people at work change or tempt you to change your attitude toward your work or the way you do your work?

6. What are the risks of being identified as one who follows God in your job? What are the benefits?

7. How might you as a Christian cultivate a culture of integrity at your workplace?

SUMMARY

Most of us find ourselves working for managers and employers who do not acknowledge or comply with the values of the Kingdom of God, or give assent to our faith or worldview. This is not an excuse to compromise our faith, or our behavior. The ethics and challenges of each of our situations are unique, and we need to determine before God the best way to honor God in our workplace with the wisdom, knowledge, and understanding he has blessed us with.

If God calls you to stay where you are, remain there and do your work with integrity. If and when God opens a new opportunity for you, continue to work with integrity there. Wherever you work, may you be known as one whom nobody can find fault with, unless it has something to do with the law of God.

MICAH 6:8

He has shown you, O man, what is good. And what does the Lord require of you? To act justly and to love mercy and to walk humbly with your God.

APPLYING GOD'S TRUTHS

What do you need to do at work to maintain a reputation like Daniel's? Share one thing with a friend.

PRAYER

Heavenly Father, we are surrounded by many temptations at work to cheat, to lie, to steal, to swear, or to be "nice guys" and compromise a little, or to behave in ways dishonorable in your eyes.

Forgive us for the times when we've succumbed to these temptations. Fill us with your Spirit, so that we can act justly and show mercy towards our co-workers and our employer. Help us to walk humbly before you, so that no one can find any fault in the way we do our work. Amen.

Chapter 5
Standing Firm in Our Faith

WHAT COST ARE WE WILLING TO PAY TO STAND FIRM IN OUR FAITH?

Be on your guard; Stand firm in the faith; be courageous;
be strong. Do everything in love.
—1 Corinthians 16:13-14

Ice Breaker:
When you were a child, what were you most afraid of?

How do we stand firm in our faith when it might cost us our job or our reputation?

God was with Daniel when he chose not to defile himself with the food of the Babylonians. God revealed to Daniel the mystery of both of King Nebuchadnezzar's dreams. God protected Daniel in the fiery furnace. God enabled Daniel to interpret what the finger of God wrote on King Belshazzar's wall.

The interpretation of these dreams and the phrase on the wall were warnings from God, and Daniel did not shirk from stating what God was going to do. Daniel always made sure to acknowledge God. Once again, Daniel faces a situation where his career and life was in jeopardy yet he chose to trust in the Lord.

DANIEL 6:6-11

So these administrators and satraps went as a group to the king and said: "May King Darius live forever! The royal administrators, prefects, satraps, advisers and governors have all agreed that the king should issue an edict and enforce the decree that anyone who prays to any god or human being during the next thirty days, except to you, Your Majesty, shall be thrown into the lions' den. Now, Your Majesty, issue the decree and put it in writing so that it cannot be altered—in

accordance with the law of the Medes and Persians, which
cannot be repealed." So King Darius put the decree in writing.

Now when Daniel learned that the decree had been
published, he went home to his upstairs room where the win-
dows opened toward Jerusalem. Three times a day he got
down on his knees and prayed, giving thanks to his God, just
as he had done before. Then these men went as a group and
found Daniel praying and asking God for help.

Around the same time as these events occurred, in Daniel chapter 9 we get a glimpse into Daniel's prayer life. Sev-
enty years prior, Jerusalem had been destroyed, and the Jews
had been carried into exile in Babylon. In the midst of his busy
life as a senior government official, Daniel found the time to
study scripture and understood from Jeremiah's prophecy that
this was the time for the Jews to return to Jerusalem (Jeremiah
25:8–14, 29:10).

DANIEL 9:4–6

I prayed to the Lord my God and confessed:
"Lord, the great and awesome God, who keeps his covenant
of love with those who love him and keep his commandments,
we have sinned and done wrong. We have been wicked and
have rebelled; we have turned away from your commands and
laws. We have not listened to your servants the prophets, who
spoke in your name to our kings, our princes and our ances-
tors, and to all the people of the land.

DANIEL 9:17-23

"Now, our God, hear the prayers and petitions of your ser-
vant. For your sake, Lord, look with favor on your desolate
sanctuary. Give ear, our God, and hear; open your eyes and
see the desolation of the city that bears your Name. We do not
make requests of you because we are righteous, but because of
your great mercy. Lord, listen! Lord, forgive! Lord, hear and
act! For your sake, my God, do not delay, because your city and
your people bear your Name."

While I was speaking and praying, confessing my sin
and the sin of my people Israel and making my request to the
Lord my God for his holy hill—while I was still in prayer,
Gabriel, the man I had seen in the earlier vision, came to
me in swift flight about the time of the evening sacrifice. He
instructed me and said to me, "Daniel, I have now come to
give you insight and understanding. As soon as you began to
pray, a word went out, which I have come to tell you, for you
are highly esteemed."

STUDY QUESTIONS

1.   Despite all his responsibilities as a senior government
     official, and the subtle plotting of his jealous co-work-
     ers, Daniel regularly and consistently studied Scrip-
     ture and prayed. Why would Daniel have chosen to
     prioritize Bible study and prayer in his life, when he
     was in a foreign country where nobody believed in
     God, and his homeland was in ruins?

2. From Daniel 6, what did Daniel pray for?

3. From Daniel 9, what characteristics of God did Daniel appeal to in his prayer? How might these characteristics of God be applicable in your work situation?

4. What did prioritizing prayer and Bible study do for Daniel, other than getting him thrown into a lion's den? What might prioritizing prayer and Bible study do for you?

5. Have you ever faced a situation similar to Daniel's? How did you respond? If you haven't, how might you respond to a situation like this?

6. What promises from God would you cling to if you were to face a situation like Daniel's?

7. Daniel had seen God repeatedly answer his prayers— sometimes quite dramatically. Share some examples of when you have seen God's faithfulness in your life, or examples of when you have seen God's care and protection in your life, or answered prayer? How do you know that God will be faithful to you in what you're facing today?

8. In the New Testament, Jesus talks about building our lives on a solid rock, so that when the storms come, we are able to stand firm. What foundations do you need to build into your life now, so that when a situation like Daniel faced comes into your life you are able to stand firm?

SUMMARY

Just as it's important to do your work with excellence, it is equally important to prioritize time for being deeply rooted in the Bible and to be aware of what God is doing around you to build his Kingdom. Daniel had cultivated a deep love relationship with God, had proven God's faithfulness, and now nothing could shake him. He was not afraid! As we balance these priorities in our lives, we will find the courage and the strength to stand firm in whatever struggles or challenges we may find ourselves in.

2 THESSALONIANS 2:15-17 (MSG)

So, friends, take a firm stand, feet on the ground and head high. Keep a tight grip on what you were taught, whether in personal conversation or by our letter. May Jesus himself and God our Father, who reached out in love and surprised you with gifts of unending help and confidence, put a fresh heart in you, invigorate your work, enliven your speech.

APPLYING GOD'S TRUTHS

What one thing do you need to do to strengthen the foundation of your life so that you will be able to stand firm in your faith?

PRAYER

Father, thank you for your word, and how you have revealed yourself to us in your word. Thank you for your rich and precious promises. We praise you because we know that you have been and will be faithful to all your promises.

Thank you for the gift of prayer, and that we can come to you at any time, in any circumstances, and that you hear and answer prayer. Thank you for the way you have answered our prayers. Thank you for your love. Thank you for your mercy.

Hear our prayers and act! Fill us with courage and strength to stand firm in the midst of all the pressures we face at work. Amen.

Chapter 6
Preparing for the Future

WHAT COULD WE DO TO PREPARE FOR TOMORROW?

But seek first his kingdom and his righteousness,
and all these things will be given to you as well.
—Matthew 6:33

Ice Breaker:
If you had unlimited money, time, energy, and abilities,
what would your dream be for your future?

WHATEVER HAPPENS NEXT IN YOUR LIFE IS TOTALLY UNDER GOD'S
control, and is not a surprise to Him. He has blessed you with
the talents and skills to handle each new situation. He will not
allow you to be tempted beyond what you are able in any new
situations that arise. God is preparing you right now for what is
next in your life.

As you go through your day, what things in your life are
keeping you from worshipping and obeying God? What can you
be doing to prepare for tomorrow? Are there things you need
to stop doing, are there things you need to get rid of, are there
new skills you need to learn, are there people you need to talk
to, and are there bills that need to be paid?

What is the faithful next step that you can take?

2 CHRONICLES 14:1–8

*And Abijah rested with his ancestors and was buried in the
City of David. Asa his son succeeded him as king, and in his
days the country was at peace for ten years.*

*Asa did what was good and right in the eyes of the Lord
his God. He removed the foreign altars and the high places,
smashed the sacred stones and cut down the Asherah poles.*

*He commanded Judah to seek the Lord, the God of their an-
cestors, and to obey his laws and commands. He removed the
high places and incense altars in every town in Judah, and
the kingdom was at peace under him. He built up the fortified
cities of Judah, since the land was at peace. No one was at
war with him during those years, for the Lord gave him rest.*

*"Let us build up these towns," he said to Judah, "and
put walls around them, with towers, gates and bars. The land
is still ours, because we have sought the Lord our God; we
sought him and he has given us rest on every side." So they
built and prospered.*

*Asa had an army of three hundred thousand men from
Judah, equipped with large shields and with spears, and two
hundred and eighty thousand from Benjamin, armed with
small shields and with bows. All these were brave fighting men.*

STUDY QUESTIONS

1. What are some of the idols people at work worship?
   What is the difference between these idols and God?

2. How can you lead by example within your sphere of
   influence at work (or at home) to tear down these
   idols?

3. After you have torn down these idols, what could you
   replace these idols with that would not be offensive to
   your co-workers or your family?

4. This passage illustrates the black-and-white choice to worship God or to worship idols. How does seeking the Lord and obeying his laws and commands at work prepare you for the future?

5. When you have times of routine and stability at work and at home, it's easy to get complacent and comfortable. What are some simple things you can do fortify your life during these quiet times for what may come in the future?

6. God gifts each one of us differently. What is the difference between how the armor of the men of Judah, and the men of Benjamin is used in battle? Were both necessary? Share an example of how you have seen the different abilities of co-workers come together to accomplish a task or project.

7. Sometimes it's easy to get frustrated with the diversity of abilities of our co-workers. What's one way you could acknowledge and appreciate the diversity of these individuals?

8. Under Asa's leadership, God raised up a large army that was always battle-ready. What new skills or abilities are you developing, or do you have, that aren't being used in your current job? How are you using these skills, or hoping to use them, someday in the future? As people share their stories, take a moment to affirm them.

SUMMARY

God has brought you to this point in your life. God is fully aware of what was happening in the world, and in your life, as you grew up. God knows the joys and heartaches you've experienced. God has been with you every step of your journey. He has blessed you with the wisdom, understanding, and knowledge to get to this point.

God says to you today, "My child, I love you. I am with you! I know what is going on. I am in control. My grace is sufficient for you today. Enjoy the blessings of this moment! As you prepare for tomorrow, remember that I have brought you to this place, and I will never leave you or forsake you. Get rid of any idols that may be hanging around, or anything else that may trip you up in the future. Choose to seek me and my kingdom and my righteousness. Embrace my commands. When tomorrow comes, I will provide you the strength to face a new day."

APPLYING GOD'S TRUTH

What is one faithful thing you can do today at work to prepare you for whatever tomorrow may bring?

PRAYER

Heavenly Father, thank you that you have been with us every day of our lives. Thank you that you will never leave us or forsake us. Forgive us for those things that have crept into our lives that keep us from worshipping you.

Thank you for the wonderful, diverse group of people you have surrounded us with, and the unique gifts you have given each one of them. Father, we place our future in your hands. Give us the wisdom to use our time today wisely today as we prepare for tomorrow. Amen.

Chapter 7

Trusting in God

WHEN OUR CIRCUMSTANCES CHANGE AT WORK, CAN WE TRUST IN GOD?

*Lord, there is no one like you to help the powerless against
the mighty. Help us, Lord our God, for we rely on you.*
—2 Chronicles 14:11

Ice Breaker:
Think of a co-worker who you trust.
Why do you trust them?

CULTIVATING AN ATTITUDE OF PRAYER DURING THE GOOD TIMES, during periods of relative of calmness and stability in our lives, gives us the boldness to come to God in prayer when life takes a twist or turn for the worse.

When you face a new situation, what's the first thing you do? Do you charge in headlong? Do you tell everybody who will listen how terrible or wonderful the situation is? Do you run and hide? Do you stop and pray and acknowledge God's sovereignty over the situation?

2 CHRONICLES 14:1, 8–15

And Abijah rested with his ancestors and was buried in the City of David. Asa his son succeeded him as king, and in his days the country was at peace for ten years…

Asa had an army of three hundred thousand men from Judah, equipped with large shields and with spears, and two hundred and eighty thousand from Benjamin, armed with small shields and with bows. All these were brave fighting men.

Zerah the Cushite marched out against them with an army of [over a million men] and three hundred chariots, and came as far as Mareshah. Asa went out to meet him, and they took up battle positions in the Valley of Zephathah near Mareshah.

Then Asa called to the Lord his God and said, "Lord, there is no one like you to help the powerless against the mighty. Help us, Lord our God, for we rely on you, and in your name we have come against this vast army. Lord, you are our God; do not let mere mortals prevail against you."

The Lord struck down the Cushites before Asa and Judah. The Cushites fled, and Asa and his army pursued them as far as Gerar. Such a great number of Cushites fell that they could not recover; they were crushed before the Lord and his forces. The men of Judah carried off a large amount of plunder. They destroyed all the villages around Gerar, for the terror of the Lord had fallen on them. They looted all these villages, since there was much plunder there. They also attacked the camps of the herders and carried off droves of sheep and goats and camels. Then they returned to Jerusalem.

STUDY QUESTIONS

1. When troubles and difficult situations occur, what's the first thing you want to do?

2. Who are the mighty people at your work? When do you feel powerless at work?

3. What does it mean to you that there is no one like the Lord to help the powerless against the mighty?

4. What gives you the confidence to rely on God? When is it hard for you to rely on God?

5. Why is it important to rely on God?

6. It is countercultural to stop and pray and acknowledge, as Asa did, our powerlessness in the face of the various situations we find ourselves in. When we acknowledge our powerlessness and believe in God's ability to help against the 'mighty,' what attributes of God are we declaring?

7. Judah had been preparing for over ten years. Yet when this army arrived, they acknowledged that they were going into battle in the name of the Lord. We don't often fight physical battles, but there are times in our lives when we face challenges and difficult situations. What does it mean to you that you can face these situations *"in the name of the Lord"*?

8. What are the alternatives to facing difficulties and challenges in life *"in the name of the Lord"*? Which would you prefer, and why?

SUMMARY

God has chosen you, and God loves you. God knows all about the situation you face, and the people you're dealing with. God is able to deal with this situation in ways you cannot believe or imagine, if you will put your trust in His infinite power and sovereignty. The people who are making your life difficult are mere mortals—no match to an immortal God. Allow God to work in this situation so that his holy name is glorified on earth and in heaven.

APPLYING GOD'S TRUTH

Before you take the next step in the situation you find yourself in, stop and acknowledge that God is in control, and ask God to help you.

PRAYER

Lord, you have proven yourself faithful to past generations, and you have proven yourself faithful to us in the past. There is no one like you to help the powerless against the mighty.

Help us, Lord our God, for we rely on you. In your name, Lord, we confidently walk into this situation, knowing you will never leave us or forsake us. Lord, you are our God; do not let these people prevail against you. Amen.

Chapter 8
Self-Reliance

Who are You Trusting to See You Through?

The path of the righteous is like the morning sun,
shining ever brighter till the full light of day.
—Proverbs 4:18

Ice Breaker:
Ask if anybody has a story they can share about
when they were drifting in a boat.

WHEN DO WE PUT OUR TRUST IN GOD, AND WHEN DO WE TRUST ourselves, or other people? This is a black-and-white question. On the one hand, it's easy to say, "Trust in the Lord with all your heart and lean not on your own understanding" (Proverbs 3:5–6), or be like the Bereans and search the Scripture daily to see if what you're hearing is true (Acts 17:11). On the other hand, we also see God expecting us to use the wisdom, understanding, and knowledge he has given us. For example, he entrusts us to take care of the earth; and we see Jesus handing over the responsibility to build the church to people like you and me.

We could say we're just going to trust in God when we're sick, and that we don't need doctors—but that negates the gifts and talents God has given doctors. Or we could say that we're just going to trust in the doctor (as King Asa does in this story), but that fails to acknowledge who provided the doctor with the wisdom to heal us.

If there isn't a simple formula as to how and when and where we should place our trust, are we just left to blindly muddle our way through, getting it right only some of the time? Or is there another way to live?

Who needs God when they have a credit card? Do you find your co-workers' attitudes towards life and work are rubbing off on you? Have you ever compromised what you believe? When do you choose to trust in God?

BACKGROUND

Asa was King of Judah. When he started out, he did what was good and right in the eyes of the Lord. He commanded Judah to seek the Lord and to obey God's laws and commands. Several years later, the King of Ethiopia attacked Judah with an army of over a million people. King Asa prayed to God, *"Lord there is no one like you to help the powerless against the mighty. Help us, Lord our God, for we rely on you and in your name we have come against this vast army. Do not let mere mortals prevail against you."* In answer to his prayer, God resoundingly crushed the Ethiopian army.

Many years later toward the end of his reign, King Asa faced a similar situation and once again he had to make a choice…

2 CHRONICLES 16:1-14

In the thirty-sixth year of Asa's reign Baasha king of Israel went up against Judah and fortified Ramah to prevent anyone from leaving or entering the territory of Asa king of Judah.

Asa then took the silver and gold out of the treasuries of the Lord's temple and of his own palace and sent it to Ben-Hadad king of Aram, who was ruling in Damascus. "Let there be a treaty between me and you," he said, "as there was between my father and your father. See, I am sending you silver and gold. Now break your treaty with Baasha king of Israel so he will withdraw from me."

Ben-Hadad agreed with King Asa and sent the commanders of his forces against the towns of Israel. They conquered Ijon, Dan, Abel Maim and all the store cities of Naphtali. When Baasha heard this, he stopped building Ramah and abandoned his work. Then King Asa brought all the men of Judah, and they carried away from Ramah the stones and timber Baasha had been using. With them he built up Geba and Mizpah.

At that time Hanani the seer came to Asa king of Judah and said to him: "Because you relied on the king of Aram and not on the Lord your God, the army of the king of Aram has escaped from your hand. Were not the Cushites and Libyans a mighty army with great numbers of chariots and horsemen? Yet when you relied on the Lord, he delivered them into your hand. For the eyes of the Lord range throughout the earth to strengthen those whose hearts are fully committed to him. You have done a foolish thing, and from now on you will be at war."

Asa was angry with the seer because of this; he was so enraged that he put him in prison. At the same time Asa brutally oppressed some of the people.

The events of Asa's reign, from beginning to end, are written in the book of the kings of Judah and Israel. In the thirty-ninth year of his reign Asa was afflicted with a disease in his feet. Though his disease was severe, even in his *illness he did not seek help from the Lord, but only from the physicians. Then in the forty-first year of his reign Asa died and rested with his ancestors. They buried him in the tomb that he had cut out for himself in the City of David. They laid him on a bier covered with spices and various blended perfumes, and they made a huge fire in his honor.*

STUDY QUESTIONS

1. What choices did King Asa make at the end of his life that were different from the choices he made after he became King? What do you think may have happened to cause him to make these choices?

2. Share a story of how you responded to challenges and difficulties in your life when you first became a Christian.

3. Today, where do you usually turn for advice or assistance when you face a challenge with a co-worker or client, or have a difficult workplace problem to solve? Why?

4. What insight might God have into these challenges? What would be the cost of turning to God for advice or assistance?

5. When do you choose to trust in yourself, when do you choose to trust in other people, and when do you choose to trust in God?

6. We hear many kinds of messages at work from non-biblical worldviews. What are some of the messages or attitudes towards life, work, raising a family, or money you hear that are different from what you believe? Which of these messages or attitudes do you find yourself believing and following? Why?

7. Share an example of when you chose to trust in the Lord, to let your confidence rest in Him. How did this choice affect your relationships at work, and the way you do your work?

8. What biblical truths give you the courage to live out your trust in the Lord even when this leads to behav ior that is different than your co-workers', or is differ ent from what society expects?

SUMMARY

PROVERBS 4:18–27

The path of the righteous is like the morning sun,
*   shining ever brighter till the full light of day.*
But the way of the wicked is like deep darkness;
*   they do not know what makes them stumble.*
My son, pay attention to what I say;
*   turn your ear to my words.*
Do not let them out of your sight,
*   keep them within your heart;*

for they are life to those who find them
    and health to one's whole body.
Above all else, guard your heart,
    for everything you do flows from it.
Keep your mouth free of perversity;
    keep corrupt talk far from your lips.
Let your eyes look straight ahead;
    fix your gaze directly before you.
Give careful thought to the paths for your feet
    and be steadfast in all your ways.
Do not turn to the right or the left;
    keep your foot from evil.

APPLYING GOD'S TRUTHS

Think of a situation you find yourself in right now. What would be a way to respond to this situation that reflects your trust in yourself or others? What would be a way to respond to this situation that reflects your trust in God?

How are you going to choose to respond to this situation, and why? Who will hold you accountable to this choice?

PRAYER

Lord, forgive us. We praise you for walking with us through the challenges and joys of life. Forgive us today for relying on our own strength, relying on our credit cards, relying on our own wisdom and abilities, and not trusting you.

As we turn our eyes back on you, Lord, we ask you to continue to be a light to our paths, and a lamp to our feet. Help us to keep your word within our heart. Guard our hearts. Help us to shine brightly like the morning sun in this dark world. Amen.

FOR FURTHER REFLECTION

The following homilies from a bygone era remind us that every generation has wrestled with calling, vocation, and Christian living. May these excerpts from F. B. Meyer be an encouragement to you.

EXODUS 31:2
I HAVE CALLED BY NAME BEZALEEL.
F. B. MEYER – OUR DAILY HOMILY

We lightly speak of a man's occupation as his calling, and fail to realize the profound significance of the phrase. One man is called to the ministry; another to the bar; others, like Bezaleel and Aholiab, to work in all manner of workmanship. Each should realize, therefore, that faculty, desire, circumstance, constitute a Divine call, and that there may be as distinct a vocation in the merchant's office, the tradesman's shop, or in the work of a domestic servant, as in the Church itself.

The morning bell that summons us to daily duty is the call of our Father, bidding us to engage in the toils to which He has assigned us. He, who gave Moses the plan, gave the artificers the power to work it in gold, silver, brass, and wood. Let this be your faith; and each morning, as you go to your work, however distasteful it may be, say, "God has called me to this; and He will fill me with all the strength, wisdom, and grace, that I need for its right doing."

Abide in your calling. — Unless it is a wrong or dishonorable one, it is better to stay in it than to become restless and changeable; and if you must leave it, wait for God to open another door.

Find in God the makeweight to all the deficiencies of your life. — If you are enslaved by daily duty, remember that in Christ you are free; if free from daily toil, in Christ you are a slave. The supply of every deficiency, the rectification of every hardship, is to be found in Jesus.

Mind to do all for God. — To do all in God and for Him, remembering that He sees and accepts all, not according to the results accomplished, but to the heavenly and holy motives that prompt the worker — this is to be blessed.

EXODUS 35:35
TO WORK ALL MANNER OF WORKMANSHIP. (R.V.)
F. B. MEYER – OUR DAILY HOMILY

There was an infinite variety in the contributions made to the Tabernacle, from the precious jewels of the rulers to the acacia wood of the poor, and the goats' hair of the women. The completed structure was a monument of the united gifts, handicrafts, and gems of the entire people. But in all there was the unity of the spirit, and plan, and devotion.

In the Church and the world there is a work for each of us to do. — It may be a very humble part in the great factory — like minding the lift, or stoking the furnace, or fetching materials for the more skilled operatives; but there is a berth for each willing worker, if only the will and way of God are diligently sought and followed.

This work is suited to our special powers. — He who prepares the work for the worker, prepares the worker for the work. Whenever God gives us a task to fulfil, it is because He sees in us faculties for its successful and happy accomplishment, in co-operation with Himself. It is a mistake then to turn back daunted by difficulty and opposition. As Caleb and Joshua said of the possessors of Canaan, "We be well able to overcome them."

We must bring our resources and powers to God. — Willing hearts were summoned to bring their offerings to the Lord. The maker of a musical instrument knows best how to develop its waiting music, and He who created and endowed us can make the most of us. Let us not work for Him; but yield ourselves to his hand, and our members as instruments of righteousness for his service. We may differ from all others in the special character of our work; but it matters not, so long as God effects through us his purpose in our creation.

For Further Study

For additional Bible study materials please visit James Bruyn's website: www.marketplace-ministry.ca.

There are also many other resources available focused on relating Christianity to the workplace. Below is a selected set of these resources. The author is not affiliated with any of these works, but has found them valuable in exploring this topic.

Regent College – Reframe Course
a 10-session video series:

This 10-week video-based course helps Christians explore how the Bible and the power of Christ reframes our lives, and invites us to reframe our world with him.

www.marketplace.regent-college.edu/reframe/

God At Work – Living Every Day With Purpose
by Ken Costa

By using the Biblical principles that underpin his faith and applying them to the 21st century workplace of today he offers practical advice on tackling the common problems familiar to many: the work-life balance, stress, ambition, failure and disappointment.

www.godatwork.org.uk

Theology of Work Project

The Project's primary mission is to produce commentaries relating significant passages from every book of the Bible to non-church workplaces.

www.theologyofwork.org

London Institute of Contemporary Christianity
(associated with John Stott)

LICC exists to envision and equip Christians and their churches for whole-life missionary discipleship in the world. We seek to serve them with biblical frameworks, practical resources, training and models so that they flourish as followers of Jesus and grow as whole-life disciplemaking communities. They produce material like:

www.licc.org.uk/splash/index.html

Fruitfulness on the Front Line
by Mark Greene

An 8-part video series from the London Institute of Contemporary Christianity, focusing on being a mouthpiece for truth and justice in the workplace.

ABOUT THE AUTHOR

James Bruyn (BMath, MATS, CMA, PMP) is a visionary leader, writer and speaker who enjoys helping individuals integrate their faith in God with their daily life. James is passionate about connecting the rich promises of our loving Heavenly Father with the joys and challenges of living out our faith in the workplace.

James is a consultant and leadership coach for the rail industry. He has a joint honors degree in Computer Science and Accounting with over twenty-five years of experience delivering innovative technology solutions for complex business problems across multiple industries. He also holds a Master of Arts in Theological Studies. James has been involved in many aspects of ministry leadership, including church planting, young adult ministry, preaching and board leadership for churches and the Navigators of Canada. He and his wife, Susan, have three teenage children.

Visit the author at www.marketplace-ministry.ca.

MARKETPLACE BIBLE STUDIES 1
GOD WITH US AT WORK

Does your faith in Christ change the way you go about your work?

As Christians working in the marketplace, we're surrounded by competing ideas that often conflict with our Christian values and beliefs. We may work in environments where loving God with all our heart, soul, and mind is a foreign concept. How do we find joy and peace when our beliefs may not be understood or encouraged? How do we demonstrate the love of God to our coworkers and our customers?

These studies offer a guide to explore how Scripture relates to your work experiences and what God has to say about your vocation and your co-workers. Take some time over a coffee break or lunch to embark on this journey of discovery with your coworkers or friends.